Series Editor: Catherine Bowness

Free at Last

The Story of Martin Luther King

R. J. Owen

RELIGIOUS AND MORAL EDUCATION PRESS

FREE AT LAST

The Story of Martin Luther King

A black man took his son out to buy him a new pair of shoes. They went into an empty shoe shop and sat down in the front row of seats. A white shop assistant came up to them.

'If you'll move to the seats at the back, I'll be glad to help you.'

'There's nothing wrong with these seats,' replied the black man.

'You'll have to move. I can't serve you here,' continued the shop assistant.

The black man saw no point in moving to other seats when nobody else was in the shop. Anyway, he did not like the idea of people having to sit in special chairs simply because of the colour of their skin.

'We'll either buy shoes sitting here, or we won't buy shoes at all.'

'I can't serve you here,' repeated the assistant.

Father and son walked out of the shop. The son was Martin Luther King.

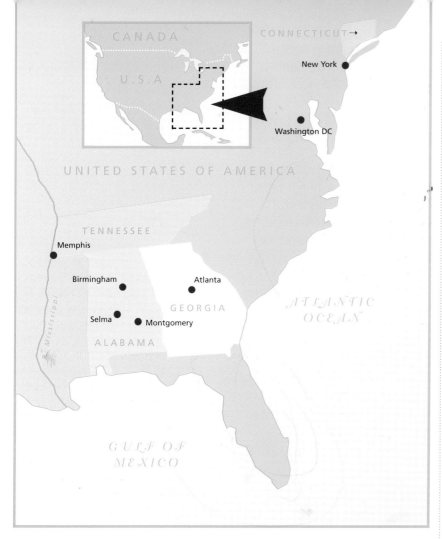

Kept Apart

As a child, Martin lived a comfortable life. His family were quite well off. He and his brother and sister always had enough to eat, good clothes to wear and a nice home.

There was only one thing wrong for Martin. He was black and he lived in a city where most white people thought black people were not as good as white ones. It was the city of Atlanta, in the southern part of the United States.

Martin was just six years old when he first learned how hard life could be for black people. Until then, his two best friends were white boys who lived nearby. They played together almost every day. However, when they were old enough to go to school, his best friends went to the school for white children. Martin had to go to the one for black children. His friends' mother kept telling him that they could not play together any more.

Martin could not understand it. He had done nothing wrong. He asked his own mother about it. Mrs King told her son all about the history of the black people in the United States. She told him about how they had been slaves and that some white people still looked down on black people and kept away from them. Mrs King tried to explain why there were many schools, cafés, cinemas, and even churches that black people could not enter. They were only for the use of white people.

'Don't let it make you feel you're not as good as white people,' said Martin's mother. 'You're just as good as anyone else, and don't you forget it.'

Martin's father was also not afraid to stand up for himself. Once, when Martin was being driven in a car by his father, a policeman stopped them.

'Boy, show me your licence!'

the policeman said to Mr King. That was the way many white people spoke to black people, even if they were grown men.

Mr King pointed to Martin. 'Do you see this child here? He's a boy. I'm a man.'

The policeman booked him. A black man was not allowed to answer back a white policeman, although the policeman could be as rude as he liked to him!

When he was fifteen years old Martin decided to find out for himself what it was like to live as an ordinary poor black person in the south of the United States. During his long summer holiday from school he took two jobs. The first one was loading and unloading parcels and goods for a railway. The second was working on the loading platform of a firm which made mattresses for beds.

The work was hard. He was able to talk to poor black people and learn about their needs. He noticed that when black people and white people were doing the same job, the whites always got paid more.

He found out what it was like to work under a white boss. The foreman at the railway, for example, never called him by his name. He just shouted out 'nigger' when he wanted him. Martin felt sure that, when he was older, he would spend a lot more time trying to get better conditions for black people.

What Do You Think?

1. Why did Martin's two childhood friends stop playing with him?

2. How do parents influence their young children? Do you think your parents still affect what you think, believe and do?

3. Why is 'looking down on' people who have a different-coloured skin unfair? For what other reasons do some people 'look down on' others?

4. Does it really matter calling another person by an unpleasant name? How do you feel when it happens to you?

His Life's Work

During his next summer holiday from school Martin worked in some tobacco fields in Connecticut. While he was there, he was asked by some of the workers to pray with them. They felt he could help them with their problems. From then on, Martin felt a stronger and stronger urge within him to be a minister of a church. He believed it was God's way of telling him that that was what He wanted.

His father was the minister of a large church in Atlanta. Religion, therefore, had always played an important part in Martin's life. He could remember and recite bits from the Bible before he was five years old. When he was only six he used to sing hymns from memory.

He liked to listen to church ministers preaching long before he was old enough to understand what they were saying. Once, when he was about ten, he said to his father, 'That man had some big words, Dad. When I grow up, I'm going to get me some big words.'

Now, as a teenager, Martin was a pupil at Morehouse College. In the United States such colleges are for teenagers. They are like our secondary schools, except that they are usually much bigger. Morehouse College had over 7000 pupils and was the best college for black students in America.

The head teacher was a man called Dr Mays. He was not a medical doctor but a church minister. When he preached he often talked about being fair to others, and about people being equal. Martin was able to see in this man both Christian faith and real concern for other people.

Martin now believed that he must help people. He wanted to solve the problems they faced in their daily lives, as well as helping them to understand the teachings of Jesus. That is why, later on, his sermons were usually about making life on earth better, as well as about God. He believed that God is a good person who fights against evil things in the world.

So when he was seventeen Martin decided that he would become a church minister. In 1948 he went to a college for those who wanted to become a minister.

It was while he was at the college that Martin first became interested in the teachings of a great Indian man, Mahatma Gandhi. Gandhi lived earlier this century. At the time, Britain ruled India. Gandhi wanted India to be free of British rule. Yet he did not believe in using violence to get rid of the British. He believed in peaceful protest, using methods like marches and strikes. Gandhi urged his followers to break unfair laws, but always to be polite and peaceful. These ideas appealed to Martin. He thought he might one day use them to get equal rights for black people in the United States.

When he had finished his training he became the minister of a Baptist church in Montgomery, Alabama.

The division between blacks and whites was very clear in Montgomery. For example, the front seats on all buses were kept for white passengers only. Even if there was nobody sitting in them and the rear seats were full, black people had to stand at the back. If the front seats were full, black people in the rear had to get up and give their seats to any white person who got on.

Black passengers had to

pay their fare at the front of the bus, get off, and walk to the rear door to get on the bus. Sometimes, after they had paid their fare, the bus would be driven off without giving them time to reach the rear door. The white drivers thought this was a great joke.

On 1 December 1955 a black woman, called Mrs Rosa Parks, got on a crowded bus. She had spent a tiring day working and shopping. She found a seat at the beginning of the black passenger section. At the next stop some white people got on. The bus-driver ordered Mrs Parks to get up and give her seat to a white man. She refused. As she said later, 'I was just plain tired, and my feet hurt.'

The driver called a policeman, who arrested her.

What Do You Think?

1. Why do you think some workers in the tobacco fields asked Martin, a teenage boy, to pray with them?

2. Martin felt an urge inside him to become a church minister. What do you think makes some young people want to do a particular job in life?

3. Dr Mays was a person whom Martin 'looked up to'. What does it mean to 'look up to' someone? What sort of person do you 'look up to'?

4. Mrs Rosa Parks broke the law. Is it ever right to break the law?

The Bus Boycott

A number of black church ministers and leaders in Montgomery met to discuss the matter. They wanted to organize a protest. It was agreed to call on all black people not to use the buses on Monday, 5 December. This was called a 'bus boycott'. On the Sunday before, in every black church, ministers appealed from their pulpits for the people to support the bus boycott.

The first bus on that Monday morning passed Martin's house at about six o'clock. Martin and his wife got up early. Martin was drinking a cup of coffee in the kitchen when it happened.

'Martin, Martin, come quickly!' his wife shouted from the living-room.

Martin rushed in.

'Look, it's empty!' she exclaimed, pointing to the passing bus.

One bus after another went by. All were empty, except for one or two white passengers. It was the same all over the city.

The bus boycott was working. For the first time, American black people had united to protest against the unfair way they were being treated. Even though some of them had to walk long distances, the black people refused to use the buses.

The leaders of the bus boycott held a meeting. They decided to call themselves the M.I.A. – the Montgomery Improvement Association. Martin was elected president. They also decided that the bus boycott would go on until the owners of the bus company changed their unfair rules. The bus boycott would cost the owners a lot of money.

That same evening thousands of black people attended a meeting called by the M.I.A. Martin, as president, was to be the main speaker. He had little time to prepare for it. Newspaper reporters and television cameras would be there. He felt nervous. He was not sure what he would say. He decided to pray for guidance.

'Lord, calm me down. Be with me now when I need your help more than ever. Help me to say the right things.'

God answered Martin's prayer. After the thousands of

Martin Luther King with his family

people had sung the hymn 'Onward! Christian Soldiers', prayed and heard a reading from the Bible, Martin spoke. He told the story of Mrs Parks. He listed some of the ways in which black people were suffering. Then he said:

'We're here this evening to say to those who have treated us wrong for so long, we're tired. Tired of being kept apart. Tired of being shamed. Tired of being kicked about.'

Everyone cheered.

'We have to protest,' continued Martin. 'We've been patient, but we come here tonight to be saved from that patience that makes us patient with anything less than freedom and fairness.'

Everyone clapped.

'But,' went on Martin, 'we must not be violent. Don't force people not to ride on the buses. Our actions must be guided by our Christian faith. Remember the words of Jesus: "Love your enemies. Bless them that curse you. Pray for them that use you badly." '

Everyone clapped and cheered.

The bus boycott went on. This was how Martin began trying to get better conditions for black people in the United States. It became known as the Civil Rights movement.

In the middle of one night Martin was wakened by the telephone ringing. He got up and picked up the receiver.

'Listen, nigger,' yelled an angry voice, 'we've taken all we want from you. Before next week you'll be sorry you ever came to Montgomery.'

It was just one of the many horrible telephone calls that Martin and his wife received. He felt he simply could not take any more. With his head in his hands, Martin prayed aloud to God: 'Lord, I'm taking a stand for what I believe is right. But I've had enough. I can't face it alone any more.'

At that moment Martin sensed that God was with him. He could not explain it. He could only feel it. Inside his mind a voice was saying, 'Stand up for what's right. Stand up for truth. God will be at your side for ever.' It was strange, but so real. Martin got up, sure that God would give him the courage to go on. He was ready to face anything now.

In the days that followed, Martin had to face many difficult times. Many threatening telephone calls were made to him. Terrible letters came by every post. One read: 'This isn't a threat but a promise – your head will be blown off, sure as Christ made green apples!'

One evening Martin was speaking at a meeting. Suddenly he noticed that some people were rushing about, looking worried.

'What's happened?' he asked a friend. His friend, Ralph, did not answer.

'Ralph, you must tell me,' said Martin.

'Your house has been bombed.'

Martin thought of his wife and young baby. 'Are Coretta and the baby all right?'

'We're checking on that now. We think so.'

His family were indeed safe, but part of the house was badly damaged. Someone had thrown a bomb into the porch. The porch had been split into two. Windows had been blown into the rooms. Broken glass covered the floors. Light bulbs were smashed. The place was a real mess. Martin rushed over to his wife. 'Thank God you and the baby are all right,' he said.

Groups of black people, angry at the bombing of their leader's home, were gathering outside. Many carried guns. Policemen were stopping people getting too near Martin's wrecked house. A policeman held back one black man who yelled, 'You got your gun. I got mine. Let's shoot it out!'

Black boys were armed with broken bottles. Some of the older black people started insulting the police. They yelled and booed. The police began to threaten the black crowd. Trouble could have flared up at any moment.

Martin went out to talk to them all. When they saw him, everyone went quiet. In a calm voice he said, 'My wife and my baby are all right. I want you to go home and put down your weapons.'

One black man shouted out, 'Aw right, Reverend, if you say so. But ah still thinks we oughta kill a few of 'em!'

'We can't solve anything by violence,' Martin went on. 'We must meet hate with love. Remember, if I am stopped, this movement will not stop. For God is with this movement.'

After that, the crowd began to thin out. People went back to their homes. A white policeman was heard to mutter, 'If it hadn't been for that nigger preacher, we'd all be dead.'

What Do You Think?

1. Martin prayed for God's help and 'God answered Martin's prayer'. Does God always answer prayers?

2. Black people were treated unfairly in the United States at this time. Are there any groups of people treated unfairly in Britain today?

3. Was Martin right to continue leading a public protest when it put the lives of his wife and young baby at risk? Give reasons for your opinion.

4. Is it a good idea to 'meet hate with love'? Does it work?

5. What does this part of the story show about Martin as a person?

Success and Suffering

The bus boycott went on for over a year. Then, at the end of 1956, the United States Supreme Court made a decision. Keeping black people and white people apart on buses was against the law of the country. Black people were, of course, very happy at the decision. The bus boycott was called off. Most white people accepted the change.

Some, however, were very angry. A few even promised that black people's blood would run in the streets if they tried to sit in the front seats of buses. One letter to Martin threatened that fifty black people's houses would be burnt down, including his, if any black person sat near white passengers. On some nights, buses were stoned. Black people were dragged off buses and beaten up. One woman, who was expecting a baby, was shot in the leg. Several black people's churches and the homes of two of Martin's friends were bombed. A pile of fourteen sticks of dynamite was found just in time on the doorstep of Martin's home.

However, despite all this, the bus boycott had been a success. Black people now had the law on their side. So in 1957 Martin and others began to protest for other rights. They wanted black people to be treated as equals at all times and in all places. On 17 May, 37 000 people, black and white, took part in a Freedom March in Washington. Martin spoke to the huge crowd. He demanded that every black person, like every white one, should have the right to vote.

At that time each person who wanted to vote had to pass a test. They had to read a few sentences from a book and then explain what they had read. It was then up to the person testing them to pass or fail them. This was really a crafty way of stopping most black people from being able to vote. Many of them had never been given a good education and, in any case, the test was often not fairly done. The right to vote was what Martin wanted to fight for next.

One day, the following year, Martin was standing in a corridor outside a courtroom when a policeman came up to him.

'Move away from here! Move on!'

'I'm waiting to see my lawyer,' replied Martin.

'If you don't get the hell out of here you're going to *need* a lawyer,' snarled the policeman.

'I'm doing no harm. I'm breaking no law. I'm waiting to see my lawyer. He won't be long.'

'Boy, you done it now,' shouted the policeman angrily.

Another policeman came over. The two of them grabbed Martin, twisted his arms behind his back and pushed him down some stairs.

Martin was kicked and beaten up. He was charged with not obeying a policeman. Two weeks later he was in court. He was found guilty and given the choice of paying a fine of $10 or going to prison for fourteen days.

'Your Honour,' said Martin, 'I cannot pay a fine for an act that I did not do. I was about to go into a courtroom when two policemen pushed, twisted, choked and kicked me. I did nothing to deserve being treated like that. The black man can no longer silently suffer cruelty from the police. We cannot do so because of what we read in the Bible. We're commanded to resist evil by the God who made us all.'

Martin was ready to go to jail. However, the police chief did not want people to feel sorry for Martin or to think badly of the police. So he paid Martin's fine himself! He said it was 'to save the taxpayers the cost of feeding King for fourteen days'.

What Do You Think?

1. Why was the bus boycott successful?

2. Should people who cannot read or write properly or are mentally handicapped be allowed to vote?

3. What would you do if you were treated unfairly by a police officer?

Stabbed

In September 1958 Martin's first book was published. He went to many bookshops to sign his name in copies of his book. One day he went to a bookshop in Harlem, the Negro part of New York. He was signing his name in a copy of his book when a black woman walked up to him.

'Are you Dr King?'
'Yes, I am.'
'Luther King, I've been after you for five years.'

There was a flash of steel as the woman pulled a knife from her clothing. She plunged it into Martin's chest.

The knife was still sticking in his chest when he was taken to hospital. It was touch-and-go whether Martin would live. The point of the knife was so near his heart that the head surgeon said later, 'If he had sneezed he would have died straight away.' In order to get the knife out of his chest, two of his ribs had to be removed.

The woman who had stabbed Martin was called Mrs Curry. She was quite mad. She kept saying that church ministers had caused her a lot of trouble. She was sent to a mental hospital.

Slowly Martin got better. He and his wife felt that God had a purpose in all this. Perhaps it was a test of their faith. Perhaps it was to force Martin to rest and take things quietly for a time. Perhaps it was to help the Civil Rights movement gain more sympathy and support from white people. Perhaps it was to prepare them for something that was still to come. Certainly, believing in God helped Martin to be calm during this time of suffering.

What Do You Think?

1. How did believing in God help Martin at important times in his life?

2. Does suffering usually have a purpose?

3. Religious people often say that God is all-loving and all-powerful. If God is like that, why do you think God does not stop people suffering?

'Sit-ins' and 'Freedom Rides'

In 1960 Martin decided to give up being minister at the Baptist church in Montgomery. He wanted to give more time to the Civil Rights movement. Its headquarters was in Atlanta, so Martin became joint minister at his father's church in Atlanta.

It was in 1960 that the 'sit-in' was used as a form of protest by American Negroes. Whites who thought blacks were being treated unfairly joined with blacks taking action. Together they would

Martin Luther King and his friend Ralph Abernathy being arrested after trying to enter a restaurant where Negroes were refused service

'sit-in' at cafés and lunch counters in big city shops, where blacks and whites were supposed to be kept apart and be served in different areas. It was during these sit-ins that the song 'We Shall Overcome' first became popular. It became the song of the Civil Rights movement.

Many suffered for what they did. They had their hair pulled. They were burnt with cigarette ends. They were beaten up. Many were arrested, including Martin. He was in jail three times during 1960 and 1961.

Most sit-ins were a success. Hundreds of cafés and shops stopped keeping black and white customers apart.

However, some parts of the United States still had buses in which black people and white people could not sit together. So in 1961 the 'freedom rides' started. Groups of young people, both black and white, would get on buses going from one state to another. They would sit together, both on the buses and in the cafés along the way.

Once, in Montgomery, a mob of 300 angry whites formed a circle round a bus as it stopped. The first 'freedom rider' to get off was a white man.

'Kill the nigger-loving son of a bitch!' screamed a woman.

Men rushed in and beat the young man until he passed out and fell to the ground. He lay in the street for an hour before an ambulance could get to him.

At Anniston, Alabama, a bus was blown up with a fire-bomb. As the 'freedom riders' staggered from the blazing bus, they were beaten with iron bars.

One of the places where black people were treated worst was Birmingham, Alabama. In 1963 Martin and the Civil Rights movement decided to protest there. In April sit-ins and protest marches were held. Within a week nearly 500 black people had been arrested. On Good Friday Martin led a march and was arrested too. He was in jail for eight days.

Shortly afterwards a thousand teenagers were arrested for taking part in a youth march. On the following day another thousand children and teenagers marched. Fire-hoses were turned on them. Children were knocked flat, their clothes soaked and ripped. Police dogs were let off their leads and ran wild. They bit first one child, then another. Some of the older black people could not stand by and do nothing. They began to throw stones and bottles at the police.

There were pictures in the newspapers and on television of young people flattened by jets of water, beaten up by police and bitten by dogs. It caused a storm of angry letters and telegrams to the President of the United States – John F. Kennedy.

What Do You Think?

1. Is it right for religious people to take part in actions which disrupt life for other people?

2. How can reports in newspapers and on TV affect people's attitude to protests?

The President Helps

The President sent Burke Marshall, who was Assistant Attorney-General in charge of Civil Rights, to Birmingham to bring about peace. Peace came. Shops stopped serving blacks and whites in separate places. There were to be more jobs open to black people. All charges against the marchers were dropped. Regular meetings were to be held between black and white leaders.

Then, in August 1963, Martin led a march on Washington for 'jobs and freedom'. About a quarter of a million people – white as well as black – took part in the march. At the Lincoln Memorial Martin spoke to the vast crowd.

> **'I have a dream that my four little children will one day live in a nation where they will not be judged by the colour of their skin, but by the sort of persons they are.**
>
> **'I have a dream that one day ... all of God's children, black men and white men, Jews and Gentiles, Protestants and Catholics, will be able to join hands and sing in the words of the black people's old song, "Free at last, free at last, thank God Almighty, we are free at last." '**

The march showed America that all blacks and very many whites now believed that everyone was equal, whatever their race or colour.

Some whites, however, still thought that blacks should not be treated the same as themselves. Less than three weeks after the Washington march someone put a bomb in a church in Birmingham. It went off while the Sunday school was being held. Four young black girls were killed.

Later in 1963 President Kennedy was murdered. Martin told his wife, 'This is what's going to happen to me also.'

Martin knew he had enemies. He knew he might be shot at or stabbed at any time.

In 1964 the F.B.I. (Federal Bureau of Investigation), the American detective organization, warned Martin to be careful. It had found out that the Ku-Klux-Klan, a secret society of whites who were anti-black, were trying to hire a 'hit-man' to kill Martin for a fee of $2000.

In January 1965 Martin was standing in the entrance hall of a hotel in Selma, Alabama. A white man came up behind him and hit him on the head. Martin had a headache for several days to remind him of

The President of the United States, John F. Kennedy

the attack. A month later the F.B.I. claimed to have stopped an attempt to kill Martin in Atlanta.

Some black leaders were becoming impatient. They thought that the only way to get justice for the black people in America was to fight for it. Martin did not agree. He was determined to keep to peaceful ways, even when he was attacked.

What Do You Think?

1. Martin had a dream of a world where the colour of a person's skin would not matter. What is your dream for the future of the world?

2. In 1963 Martin told his wife that he was going to be murdered. Can people really sense or know what is going to happen in the future?

3. Was Martin brave or foolish to carry on with the Civil Rights work if he knew it would cost him his life? Is anything worth dying for?

4. Some black leaders became impatient with the slow progress towards getting equal rights. Is there ever a time or situation when violence may be the best course of action?

The Right to Vote

In the autumn of 1964 Martin was told that he had won the Nobel Peace Prize. This is an award given each year to someone who has done much to encourage peace or to stop violence. Martin went to Norway to receive the prize.

The prize was $54 000 (about £30 000). But Martin did not keep it for himself. He gave it away to several freedom movements and organizations which were trying to get equal rights for black people.

The Civil Rights movement moved to Selma. In February 1965 Martin led a march there calling for all black people to have the right to vote. He was arrested again.

In March another freedom march took place in Selma. State troopers blocked the road. The marchers were ordered to stop. They were given two minutes to turn back. Less than a minute went by before the order was given: 'Troopers, forward!' Sixty troopers charged into the unarmed marchers to the cry of 'Get those goddam niggers!'. Tear-gas grenades were thrown at the marchers. They were beaten with clubs and slashed with whips.

'March, nigger! You wanted to march and now I'm gonna help you,' screamed one trooper as he whipped a young boy. Over sixty people were injured by this cruelty.

Yet slowly black people were winning their fight for the right to be treated fairly. In August 1965 the Voting Rights Act was passed. Blacks now had the same rights as whites to vote.

What Do You Think?

1. Martin gave away all the Nobel Peace Prize money he was awarded. What does this action show about Martin?

2. If you had a large sum of money to give away, what 'good cause' would you give it to?

Martin was concerned about all aspects of fair treatment. In 1964, for example, he and other church ministers formed a picket line outside the factory of the Scripto Company in Atlanta. He supported the workers (who were mainly black) who wanted to form a union to try and better their working conditions.

Early in 1967 Martin spoke out against the Vietnam war. American soldiers were fighting with the armies of South Vietnam against North Vietnam. Martin was against American soldiers being in the war for two reasons. First, thousands and thousands of Vietnamese people, both adults and children, were being injured or killed. Second, black families and poor families in America were badly affected by the death and injury of their menfolk. Martin wanted peace and equal rights for everybody at home *and* abroad.

In 1968 Martin went to Memphis, Tennessee. He went to arrange a march in support of dustmen there. They had gone on strike because of the unfair way they were being treated by the new mayor.

Martin stayed in Room 306 of the Lorraine Motel. Opposite the motel was a rather shabby hotel. Here a man calling himself 'John Willard' rented Room 5B which overlooked the balcony of Martin's room. This man's real name was James Earl Ray, an escaped prisoner and white American who hated black people.

This man secretly took up

Martin Luther King on the balcony of Room 306 on Wednesday, 3 April 1968

to Room 5B a pair of binoculars, a rifle and a box of bullets. At about six o'clock on the evening of Thursday, 4 April, Martin stepped outside on to the balcony of the motel. He went for a breath of fresh air. Soon he would be going out to speak at a meeting.

From the street outside a friend called up, 'It's getting chilly, Dr King. Better take an overcoat with you.'

'O.K.,' Martin replied, 'I will.'

Suddenly a shot was fired from the shabby hotel opposite. Martin fell backwards. Blood gushed from a three-inch hole in his neck. His brain was damaged. His spine was broken.

He was rushed to hospital. One hour later he was dead – a victim of the violence that for so many years he had tried to stop.

Mrs King had to break the terrible news to her children. The eldest, Yoki, said, 'Mum, I'm not going to cry, because my dad's not really dead. His body's dead but his spirit will never die. I'm going to see him again in heaven.' Tears were running down her cheeks. Then she added, 'Mum, should I hate the man who killed my dad?'

'No, darling,' said Mrs King quietly, 'your dad wouldn't want you to do that.'

President Lyndon B. Johnson made the following Sunday a special day of mourning for Martin throughout the country. Important sports events were cancelled. Many television and radio programmes were changed. Martin's wife received over 150 000 letters, cards and telegrams and gifts of flowers from people from all over the world.

Many black people were angry. Yet what they did when they heard of his death was against all that Martin believed in. There were riots in some sixty American cities. On hearing that Martin had been shot dead, one black man promised to kill the first white man he saw. He got his gun, went out onto the street and did exactly what he had promised.

At the time of his death Martin and the Civil Rights movement had done much for black people. To separate blacks from whites had been made illegal. It was against the law to refuse a job or not allow a black person to rent a house simply because of his colour. The right of a black person to vote had been accepted.

Such progress continued after Martin's death. Some black people have been elected to public office. In 1973, for example, one man was elected Mayor of Los Angeles. In 1977 another, Andrew Young, became United States Ambassador to the United Nations.

In the 1980s there was a black candidate for the office of President of the United States – Jesse Jackson. At the same time Martin's son, Marty, became a City Commissioner in Atlanta – something which would have thrilled Martin.

Since 1986 the third Monday in January has been a national holiday in the United States. It is Martin Luther King Day and is on or near Martin's birthday. It is held to celebrate Martin's work in helping the United States become a more just society.

In his final speech on 3 April 1968, at Memphis, Martin spoke of threats against his life:

'Like anybody, I would like to live a long life. But I'm not concerned about that now. I just want to do God's will.'

Several times Martin had said to friends, 'I'll never live to be forty. I'll never make it.' He was thirty-nine years old when he was murdered.

Two months before he died he had said that, if ever he were killed, he would like people to say that 'Martin Luther King tried to give his life serving others'.

On his gravestone were written these words:

FREE AT LAST, FREE AT LAST

THANK GOD ALMIGHTY

I'M FREE AT LAST

Biographical Notes

Martin Luther King was born on 15 January 1929 in Atlanta, Georgia, in the heart of the American South. Educated at Atlanta University Laboratory High School, Booker T. Washington High School and Morehouse College, he went on to study at Crozer Theological Seminary in Chester, Pennsylvania. Here, in 1951, he obtained a Bachelor of Divinity degree. In 1954 Boston University awarded him the degree of Doctor of Philosophy in systematic theology.

Martin was ordained a Baptist minister in 1947, the same year as he was made assistant pastor at Ebenezer Baptist Church, Atlanta.

On 18 June 1953 he was married to Coretta Scott.

In 1954 he was called to the pastorate of the Dexter Avenue Baptist Church in Montgomery, Alabama, where he ministered until 1960. That year he became co-pastor of Ebenezer Baptist Church.

In 1957 Martin was awarded the National Association for the Advancement of Coloured People's Spingarn Medal. This was given to the person making the greatest contribution in the field of race relations. In 1964 he received the Nobel Peace Prize.

Martin Luther King was murdered on 4 April 1968 in Memphis, Tennessee. He was married, with four children (the eldest aged thirteen), when he was killed. His children are called Yolanda (Yoki), Martin (Marty), Dexter and Bernice (Bunny).

Martin Luther King's books include *Stride towards Freedom*, *Strength to Love* and *Why We Can't Wait* (all published in 1958).

Things to Do

1. Draw a large map of the United States of America. Mark on the map the outlines of the states of Alabama, Tennessee, Georgia and Connecticut; the cities of New York and Washington D.C.; and the towns of Atlanta, Montgomery, Birmingham, Selma and Memphis. Alongside the name of each town or city, write one or two sentences saying what Martin did or what happened to him there.

2. Take the letters of a key word in the story of Martin Luther King (e.g. freedom, dream, boycott, equality, non-violence). Use each letter in turn as the initial letter of another word to make up a slogan for equal rights.

3. Draw a cartoon strip showing the most important events in the story of Martin Luther King.

4. Imagine you are **either** one of Martin Luther King's children **or** a friend of his. Write a series of daily diary entries entitled 'A week in the life of Martin Luther King'. Base your entries on the information, activities and events mentioned in this book.

5. Improvise a short dramatic sketch based on **one** of the following parts of the story.

   (a) In the shoe shop (page 2)
   Characters: Martin, Martin's father, shop assistant.

   (b) Trouble on the bus (page 6)
   Characters: Mrs Rosa Parks, white man, bus-driver, policeman.

   (c) In court (pages 11 to 12)
   Characters: Martin, two policemen, judge.

6. Create a board game (such as snakes and ladders) showing the progress and set-backs experienced by black people in the United States during the 1950s and 1960s.

7. Design a poster or placard which could have been used by black people at a protest march or sit-in in the 1960s.

8 Imagine you are a newspaper reporter at **either** a Civil Rights march (see pages 14 and 16) **or** the Lorraine Motel (pages 17 to 18). Make up a headline and write a report for the front page of your newspaper. If possible, use a word-processor or DTP to print out your headline and report.

9 Fold a piece of A4 card or paper into two and design a greetings card to send to Martin Luther King's widow on Martin Luther King Day. Choose appropriate words, symbols and illustrations.

10 The Lorraine Motel in Memphis has been changed into the National Civil Rights Museum. Imagine you have been asked to open the Museum. Write a two-minute speech which you could use to open the Museum.

11 Find out about Mahatma Gandhi and his campaign of non-violence in India. Then write an account of his life as an entry in a biographical dictionary.

12 Make a collage of newspaper cuttings about individuals and groups who are 'different' in some way. Draw up a 'charter of rights' which would help such people be treated fairly and have equal rights, and use this charter as the centre-piece of your collage.

13 Think about an injustice which exists in the world today and which you feel strongly about. Write a letter to the government of that country or write a poem about this injustice.

14 Make up and illustrate a prayer for peace **or** freedom **or** equal rights.

15 Interview a minister or member of a Baptist church about the main Baptist beliefs. Before the interview, decide on a (short) list of questions and issues you would like to ask about, such as believers' baptism, church organization or the role of women in the church. Afterwards, write down an account of the interview.

Questions for Assessment or Examination Candidates

16 Research into New Testament teaching about attitudes to other races. Read Luke, chapter 7, verses 1–10; chapter 9, verses 51–55; chapter 10, verses 30–37; Acts, chapter 10, verse 1 to chapter 11, verse 18; Galatians, chapter 3, verse 28; Revelation, chapter 7, verses 9–10. Write a report on your findings.

17 Answer **one** of the following structured essays:

(a) Explain, with examples, the difference between prejudice and discrimination. (5 marks)

(b) In what ways did Martin Luther King oppose racial discrimination? (10 marks)

(c) 'Religious believers should not discriminate against other people but be free to think what they like about others.' Do you agree? Give your reasons, showing that you have thought about more than one point of view. (5 marks)

OR

(a) Explain the teaching of **one** religious tradition about prejudice and discrimination. (5 marks)

(b) Explain some of the problems a black person may face when living in a mainly white society. (10 marks)

(c) 'There is nothing more evil in Britain today than prejudice.' Do you agree? Give your reasons, showing that you have thought about more than one point of view. (5 marks)

Note A useful resource for question 11 opposite is the Faith in Action book *Man of Peace*, by Audrey Constant, which tells the story of Mahatma Gandhi.

Religious and Moral Education Press
*A division of SCM-Canterbury Press Ltd,
a subsidiary of*
Hymns Ancient & Modern Ltd
St Mary's Works, St Mary's Plain
Norwich, Norfolk NR3 3BH

First published 1980

New edition first published 1997
Reprinted 1998, 1999, 2000, 2001, 2002,
2003

ISBN 1 85175 133 5

Designed and typeset by
TOPICS – The Creative Partnership,
Exeter

Illustrations by Brian Platt

Printed in Great Britain by
Brightsea Press, Exeter for
Religious and Moral Education Press,
Norwich

Notes for Teachers

The first Faith in Action books were published in the late 1970s and the series has remained popular with both teachers and pupils. However, much in education has changed over the last twenty years, such as the development of both new examination syllabuses in Religious Studies and local agreed syllabuses for Religious Education which place more emphasis on pupils' own understanding, interpretation and evaluation of religious belief and practice, rather than a simple knowledge of events. This has encouraged us to amend the style of the Faith in Action Series to make it more suitable for today's classroom.

The aim is, as before, to tell the stories of people who have lived and acted according to their faith, but we have included alongside the main story questions which will encourage pupils to think about the reasons for the behaviour of our main characters and to empathize with the situations in which they found themselves. We hope that pupils will also be able to relate some of the issues in the stories to other issues in modern society, either in their own area or on a global scale.

The 'What Do You Think?' questions may be used for group or class discussion or for short written exercises. The 'Things to Do' at the end of the story include ideas for longer activities and more-structured questions suitable for assessment or examination practice.

In line with current syllabus requirements, as Britain is a multifaith society, Faith in Action characters will be selected from a wide variety of faith backgrounds and many of the questions may be answered from the perspective of more than one faith.

CMB, 1997

Acknowledgements
The publishers would like to thank the original General Editors of the Faith in Action Series, Geoffrey Hanks and David Wallington, for their contribution to the development of the first edition of this book.

Photographs are reproduced by kind permission of Associated Press Ltd (page 17), Pixfeatures (page 8) and Popperfoto (page 13).